Harold Boulton

Songs Sung and Unsung

Harold Boulton

Songs Sung and Unsung

ISBN/EAN: 9783337019976

Printed in Europe, USA, Canada, Australia, Japan

Cover: Foto ©Thomas Meinert / pixelio.de

More available books at **www.hansebooks.com**

SONGS

SUNG AND UNSUNG

BY

HAROLD BOULTON.

LONDON:
The Leadenhall Prefs, Ltd: 50, Leadenhall Street, E.C.
Simpkin, Marshall, Hamilton, Kent & Co., Ltd:

New York: Charles Scribner's Sons, 743 & 745, Broadway.

THE LEADENHALL PRESS, LTD:
50, LEADENHALL STREET, LONDON, E.C.
T 4,652.

THANKS ARE DUE FOR PERMISSION
TO RE-PUBLISH
POEMS IN "SONGS SUNG"
TO
MESSRS. ASHDOWN & CO.,
MR. CHARLES BETHUNE,
MESSRS. BOOSEY & CO.,
MESSRS. CASSELL & CO., LIMITED,
MESSRS. CHAPPELL & CO.,
MESSRS. ROBERT COCKS & CO.,
MESSRS. J. B. CRAMER & CO.,
THE LEADENHALL PRESS, LIMITED,
AND MESSRS. NOVELLO, EWER & CO.

Preface to Songs Sung.

THE bringing together of lyrics that have been published at various times and with music by various composers will, it is hoped, be of interest to those who have *set* and those who have *sung* them. For the writer himself this re-publication awakens mingled memories. Happy thoughts of early friendships and echoes of melodious hours long past are unavoidably associated with sorrowful regrets for composers and singers on whom the silence of death too soon has fallen.

But the work of all concerned remains in evidence.

Not a few of the airs to which these words are mated have won such favour as to throw considerable lustre on the partnership. Those who find a temporary disunion of words and music distasteful have the remedy in their own hands.

H. B.

INDEX.

SONGS SUNG.

From "TWELVE LYRICS."

	COMPOSER.	PAGE.
Time's Garden	Arthur Goring Thomas	13
Voices of Spring	” ” ”	14
A Song of Sunshine	” ” ”	15
The Viking's Daughter	” ” ”	16
The Heart's Fancies	” ” ”	17

From "TWELVE NEW SONGS."

For Ever Mine	C. V. Stanford	18
In Summer Weather	Charles H. Lloyd	19
Constancy	Sir Joseph Barnby	20
Robin Sly	A. C. Mackenzie	21
A Song of the South	Hamish MacCunn	23
The Maid of Elsinore	C. Hubert Parry	24
To Welcome You	Arthur Goring Thomas	26
Cradle Song	Alfred Cellier	27
A Pretty Maid	Arthur Somervell	28
Love's Journey	F. Corder	29
Truant Wings	Frederic Cowen	30
The Windflower	Charles Wood	31

From "SEVEN SONGS TO SING."

	COMPOSER.	PAGE
Still Present	Lord Henry Somerset	32
Barcarolle	Theo. Marzials	33
Last Words	Malcolm Lawson	34
Alas and Alack-a-day Me!	Cotsford Dick	35
"Leave Me No More"	L. Denza	37
Pipe and Tabor	J. L. Roeckel	38
Life's Devotion	Alfred Caldicott	40

From "SONGS OF THE NORTH."

Maiden of Morven	Malcolm Lawson	41
Skye Boat Song	,, ,,	43
Lament for Maclean of Ardgour	,, ,,	45

From "SONGS OF THE FOUR NATIONS."

Pretty Polly Oliver	Arthur Somervell	47
The Mackintosh's Lament	,, ,,	49
All Through the Night	,, ,,	50
The Castle of Dromore	,, ,,	51
The Tree in the Wood; or, Young Denis	,, ,,	52

From "EIGHT VOCAL DUETS."

Tears	Theo. Marzials	54
Light Vows	,, ,,	55

From "MAYTIDE IN MY GARDEN."

The Coming of May	Frederic Cowen	56
Voices in the Garden	,, ,,	58
Morning Flow'rets	,, ,,	59
Mayday and Maynight	,, ,,	60
Falling Blossoms	,, ,,	61
Elegy	,, ,,	62

From "Twelve Songs."

	COMPOSER.	PAGE.
The Voice of the Wind	Theo. Marzials	63
None the Less	,, ,,	64
The Rosebud	,, ,,	66
A Song of Gladness	,, ,,	67

Miscellaneous.

Love will Endure	Alfred Scott-Gatty	68
Gillian	Charles Bethune	69
"Thoughts of You"	Tivadar Nachez	70
Irish Spinning Song	Arthur Somervell	71
Love the Harvester	Alfred Cellier	73

SONGS SUNG.

ERRATA.

Page 51 for "ill-winds" read ill-will

,, 64 ,, "yoeman" ,, yeoman

,, 71 ,, "who" ,, whom

SELECTIONS FROM "TWELVE LYRICS"

(Set to Music by Arthur Goring Thomas)

Time's Garden.

THERE is a garden hidden
    Beyond this troubled clime,
Where wounded hearts are bidden
    To heal their hurts of Time.

Not that their hearts can harden
    Whose passion's vows were true,
But, like the flowers of that garden,
    They bud and bloom anew.

To the banks of a dreamy river,
    'Mid poppies and asphodels,
Time, gentle-handed driver,
    His piteous team compels.

There, till their thirst is over,
    He sings to each anon,
"Rest, broken-hearted lover,
    And drink oblivion."

Voices of Spring.

WHO'S for Lent lillies and daffadowndillies?
    Who'll to the wood where a thousand birds sing?
There whom it pleases shall feel the light breezes
    Thrill the heart's blood with the glamour they bring.

Come old and crusty, come lovers lusty,
    Maids must be wooed with a kiss and a ring;
Old earth rejoices to hear your glad voices,
    Life, life is good, for at last it is spring.

A Song of Sunshine.

CHURL winter his flight has taken,
　　The green buds are opening;
My lover awaken,
　　And walk abroad in the spring.

The thrush leads the choir
　　In leafy citadel;
The wren, like a little brown friar,
　　Has his homely tale to tell.

" Let every creature
　　Love life and liberty."
This creed the small hedge-preacher
　　Proclaims from tree to tree.

Come then ! 'Tis spring, 'tis maytime,
　　And the glad day just begun;
Sweetheart, 'tis playtime.
　　Come out into the sun.

The Viking's Daughter.

IT was a Viking's daughter,
   As fair as fair could be,
Sat wondering at the water,
   Beside the summer sea.

But as she fell to sleeping,
   The white waves crept around,
And bore her in their keeping
   Beneath the surging sound.

In vain her lover sought her
   Along the weary shore :
There lies the Viking's daughter,
   Asleep for evermore.

The Heart's Fancies.

I DREAMED my heart was a blossom
   That grew in a garden fair,
You laid it upon your bosom,
   And it bloomed for ever there.

I thought my heart was a lyre
   You played soft airs upon,
And then I thought it a fire
   Whose radiance warm'd your own.

You know my heart is a true heart,
   By love half worn away;
Your love would make it a new heart
   For ever and a day.

"TWELVE NEW SONGS,"
BY TWELVE BRITISH COMPOSERS.

For Ever Mine.

(Set to Music by C. V. STANFORD)

I LIKEN my love to a gossamer
  Afloat in the summer air,
And wish that I were the west wind,
  Her form on my wings to bear ;
  She is so daintly delicate,
    So pure, so rare.

I liken my love to a butterfly,
  By a bower of roses flown,
The flowers my fellows are sleeping,
  And I am awake alone ;
  I open my petals to welcome her
    To her fairy throne.

I liken my love to a hundred things
  In the realm of fancy fine,
Wherein I follow and woo her,
  In the core of my heart to twine.
  Oh ! May she peacefully nestle there,
    For ever mine !

In Summer Weather.

(Set to Music by CHARLES H. LLOYD)

THERE'S tender green on the tree,
   The birds are in finest feather,
And lovers in ecstasy
   Go wandering forth together.
Sing heigh ! Sing ho ! How the merry days go
   In the first of the summer weather !

The bird must capture his mate,
   By sweet conpulsion driven,
And Colin will steal from Kate
   The kisses for which he's striven.
Sing heigh ! Sing ho ! But the rogue must know
   How quickly he'll be forgiven !

Then seize the prime o' the time,
   That your fruit be rich and mellow ;
And warble your love in rhyme,
   Ere the leaf be sere and yellow.
Sing heigh ! Sing ho ! 'Tis a world of woe,
   Till everyone find his fellow.

Constancy.

(Set to Music by Sir Joseph Barnby)

My heart that burns like the noon-tide
    Has waited the long day through,
And still in the gloaming I long for your coming,
    As flowers faint for the dew.

Oh! Come in the cool of the evening
    Like a soft wind out of the west;
Oh! Come like the swallow that flies o'er the fallow
    Homeward at night to the nest.

The nightingale in the garden
    Cries "Look, look, look, truant love,
The pale stars glimmer, the moonbeams shimmer,
    And glide through the leaves above."

Ah me! But the midnight passes,
    I linger and know not why;
Though you came never, I hope for ever,
    A lover must hope or die.

Robin Sly.

(A COUNTRY BALLAD)

(Set to Music by A. C. MACKENZIE.)

IN the shade sits Robin Sly,
    Waiting there till Kate comes by;
Lovers' quarrel has been rife,
Robin vows that ere it ends
Kate must kiss and make amends.
    "Wilful maid makes shrewish wife."
So says Robin, wise Sir Robin,
    Brave Robin Sly.

But while Robin sits sedate,
Who comes through the wicket gate?
    Who but Kate and Ploughman Joe?
Kate that laughs at Robin Sly,
Singing as she passes by,
    "Let him cool a year or so."
Angry Robin, wistful Robin,
    Sad Robin Sly!

Joe the happiest husband thrives,
Kate the most discreet of wives ;
    So it is that in the wooing
Maids must have the mastery,
Men must wait till by-and-bye ;
    Learning this was thy undoing,
Hasty Robin, foolish Robin,
        Poor Robin Sly !

A Song of the South.

(Set to Music by Hamish Macunn)

I HAVE a garden beautiful,
  By a sea of peerless blue ;
There are sunny slopes and grottoes cool,
  And a streamlet wanders through.

There are oranges and cypresses,
  There are vines and olives grey,
And soft winds rustling through the trees
  That whispering seem to say :

"Come to my bounteous Paradise,
  My Eden of the South,
Come with the love-light in your eyes,
  Warm kisses on your mouth."

Thrilled by the flower-scented gale,
  The sea and sky of blue,
My trembling pulses start and fail,
  And faint, dear heart, for you.

Shine through the air, a vision fair,
  And make my dream come true !

The Maid of Elsinore.

(Set to Music by C. Hubert Parry)

A TEARFUL boy king Olaf stood,
   'Mid his warriors grim and grey,
As the good ship bore him over the flood,
   From his first fond love away.
His wistful eyes still sought the shore,
   But his rough Earls laughed that Odin's seed
The woodland flower should stoop to heed,
     —The Maid of Elsinore.

The mountain pine grows strong and sure,
   By northern tempest swayed,
The frail hare-bell will bloom secure
   In the sheltered forest glade ;
Thus Olaf's arm waxed great in war,
   Till distant isles his prowess knew,
And fairer bloomed and ever true
     The Maid of Elsinore.

'Twas ten long years of storm and fight
    By many a foreign main,
Ere great King Olaf's conquering might
    Came sailing home again ;
The Viking ships were ranged ashore,
    The rough Earls laughed in scorn no more,
He placed her hands within his own,
    Upon her brow the Queenly crown ;
O'er fiord and field the glad bells pealed
        For the Maid of Elsinore.

To Welcome You.

(Set to Music by ARTHUR GORING THOMAS)

THERE are faces peeping out of all the flowers,
    And the little buds are wakeful every one,
With their pretty lips that pout at chilly showers,
    And open with a smile to kiss the sun.

There are voices sweet and low among the rushes
    That the ripples of the river gently shake,
There's a murmuring among the alder bushes,
    As the wind is wafted gently o'er the lake.

To-day I hear the voices full of singing,
    The flower-faces smile and whisper too,
The whole wide world with melody is ringing,
    And all, my heart of hearts, to welcome you.

Cradle Song.

(Set to Music by ALFRED CELLIER)

SLEEP child, and may thy cradle be
   A ship upon a halcyon sea,
Gliding with silver sail unfurled
Beyond the turmoil of the world.
Sing tenderly, tenderly,
" Lullaby, lullaby."

Oh! Drift into some drowsy bay,
Where only quiet dreams hold sway,
Where healing herbs no pain allow,
Where golden birds on bended bough
Sing soothingly, soothingly,
" Lullaby, lullaby."

Then wake, my babe, and step ashore
Into thy mother's arms once more ;
And may life's journeys ever end
Upon the bosom of a friend.
Sing tenderly, tenderly,
" Lullaby, lullaby."

A Pretty Maid.

(Set to Music by ARTHUR SOMERVELL.)

A PRETTY maid went a-maying,
   And roamed the fields afar;
And everywhere she went,
With all the world content,
She heard the song-birds saying:
"How pretty, dear, you are."

Her lap with flow'rs was laden,
She rested by a brook;
She saw her face below,
And 'mid the water's flow
A voice said to the maiden:
"How pretty, dear, you look."

Her true love stood beside her,
She did not say him nay;
But still, as in a dream,
She gazed into the stream,
While he with fond words plied her,
And stole her heart away.
"Pretty pretty dear, I've lov'd you for a year,
I'll marry you when I may."

Love's Journey.

(Set to Music by F. Corder)

❦

MOONBEAM purest and serenest,
That from Heaven's pale vapour leanest,
Shining earthward, far away,
With thy lustrous silver ray,
Shine on my beloved's home,
Tell her swift as thee I come.

Dawning sun, thou orb of wonder,
Rolling sable clouds asunder,
Shake the dun mist from thy brow,
Rim with gold her dwelling now ;
Tell her, glorious messenger,
How I haste to come to her.

Night's long journeyings are over,
I am come to thee, dear lover ;
Here I wait at earliest dawn,
'Mid the roses on thy lawn ;
Open wide thy window, Sweet,
I am kneeling at thy feet.

Truant Wings.

(Set to Music by FREDERIC COWEN)

COME, swallow, come, for thee we wait;
  Come seek thy northern home anew,
Where pale spring-flowers are delicate,
  And winter skies are changed to blue.
    Come, swallow, come, for thee we wait.

Come, swallow, come, for thee we wait;
  The thatch is warm beneath the sun,
Here tell of love to thy fond mate,
  To-day should see thy nest begun.
    Come, swallow, come, for thee we wait.

Come, swallow, come, for thee we wait;
  The spring is perfect but for thee,
Ah! Welcome, though thou speedest late
  Thy truant wings from o'er the sea.
    Welcome, for not in vain we wait.

The Windflower.

(Set to Music by CHARLES WOOD)

ERE buds and blades are springing,
Or swallows northward winging,
The white windflower appears.

In many an upland valley
And frostbound woodland alley
Her star-like head she rears.

The cold east wind hath kissed her,
The snowflakes call her "sister,"
And nestle by her side.

So meek she lives and lowly,
So fragile, pure, and holy,
The spring's unsullied bride.

But when the hot sun showers
His strength on summer flowers,
Her short sweet life is done.

So we one day discover
Our life's first bloom is over,
Our love's first promise gone.

"SEVEN SONGS TO SING,"
BY SEVEN COMPOSERS.

Still Present.

(Set to Music by LORD HENRY SOMERSET)

O LOVE whose life to mine most dear
Hath passed from out my sight,
Now in the silent still midnight
I know that thou art near.

I feel thy hands upon my head,
Thy warm lips thrill mine own,
Thy soul in me so deep hath grown
I dare not call thee dead.

Barcarolle.

(Set to Music by THEO. MARZIALS)

THE balmy breath of twilight
   Invites us to be free ;
Come, launch our boat together,
   And sail away to sea.

We'll float along the silver track
   Beneath the bright moonbeam ;
We'll ride upon the billow's back,
   As happy as a dream.

For Hope shall ever mind the sail,
   And Love the helm attend,
Nor aught but favouring winds prevail,
   Until our journey's end.

The balmy breath of twilight
   Invites us to be free ;
Come, launch our boat together,
   And sail away to sea.

Last Words.

(Set to Music by MALCOLM LAWSON)

L IFE'S flame begins to flicker,
   The wine of life is done;
The gloom of night grows thicker,
   Ah! Let me be alone!

The past is surging o'er me,
   A half-remembered dream;
The future looms before me,
   A dark unfathomed stream.

My mortal sight grows weary,
   Farewell, thou dearest one;
The path is dim and dreary,
   And I must forth alone.

Alas and Alack-a-day Me!

(Set to Music by COTSFORD DICK)

I HEARD a maid singing "Alas and alack,"
    And weeping most sorry to see ;
"My lover is gone, he will never come back,
    Alas and alack-a-day me !

"He was fair as the day, and I was but his whim,
    He was false as a traitor could be ;
And the light of my poor little life was in him,
    Alas and alack-a-day me ! "

"Take heart, little beauty," I laughingly said,
    "There's many good fish in the sea ;
And there's lovers in plenty to woo and to wed,
    As thick as the leaves on the tree.

"So if you're contented to dry those bright eyes,
    And try a fresh hazard with me ;
We'll soon make an ending of sorrow and sighs,
    And alas and alack-a-day me ! "

She lifted her apron to dry the salt brine,
    Her face was a picture to see;
Her little hand fell like a snowflake in mine,
    And her little heart melted to me.

"You lovers," she sighed, "are a scourge and a curse,
    But women can never be free;
You may prove a better, you cannot be worse,
    Alas and alack-a-day me!"

"Leave Me No More."

(Set to Music by L. Denza)

LEAVE me no more to sorrow and sighing,
    Love's noon is fadeless and knows not of night ;
Why should we heed that daylight is dying?
    Why should we follow the hours in their flight ?
Song-birds are nestling close to the tree-top,
    Far and asunder no longer to soar ;
Now all things in nature seek shelter and slumber,
    Come rest in my haven, leave me no more.

See yonder ship sail home to the river,
    Soft from the ocean the light breezes blow ;
How like a lover, importunate ever,
    Hast'ning to meet her the glad waters flow.
Now you are near me, fain would I hold you,
    Safe as a truant ship moored to the shore ;
Then here make an ending of tempest and travel,
    Come rest in my haven, leave me no more.

Pipe and Tabor.

(Set to Music by J. L. Roeckel)

A PURITAN, severe and staid,
    To meeting-house would go,
Fell in with a merry dancing maid,
    Nimble of heel and toe.
She was lively as a butterfly,
    She was lovely as a flower;
But Brother Smite-em-hip-and-thigh
    Passed on with visage sour.
"Avaunt! Avoid! Alack-a-day!
    Beshrew me, worthy neighbour,
They dally down a red-hot way,
    That dance to pipe and tabor."

But wiles of Satan well withstood,
    Are joy to the devout;
So Brother Smite-em doth conclude
    To stop and fight it out;
While from the meeting-house there peals,
    In nasal psalmody,

"Why tarry thus the chariot-wheels
   Of Brother Hip-and-thigh?"
With " I 'certes, I 'fegs, and well-a-way,
   Beshrew me, gossip neighbour;
Yon vessel is of comely clay,
   That trips to pipe and tabor!"

There is a genial puritan,
   Of visage debonair,
Who lives, a happy married man,
   With faithful spouse and fair.
And when with meed of labour meet
   The busy day is sped,
Six rosy chicks with nimble feet
   The merry morris tread.
"Indeed, in truth, and sooth to say,
   I blame not pipe and tabor,
Nor honest mirth, nor harmless play
   With love that lightens labour."

Life's Devotion.

(Set to Music by ALFRED CALDICOTT)

ONLY one word to say,
   'Tis that I have none
Great enough, good enough,
   To greet my chosen one.
Oh! Were my love the infinite sea,
   And every wave a silver tongue,
Their soul-enrapturing harmony
   Would seem like a song half sung.

Only one thought to think,
   How to serve thee best,
Toil for thee, strive for thee,
   Live for thy behest.
At thy dear presence doubt is fled,
   The path shines clear at thy command ;
Soft sunlight hovers round thy head,
   And earth is a fairy-land.

Only one life to live :
   Would that I had more,
At thy feet to offer thee,
   Thee whom I adore.
For thine is every hour I live
   And thine alone each pulse and breath ;
If there be aught beyond to give
   I'll vow it thine in death.

Selections from "SONGS OF THE NORTH"

(Music arranged by MALCOLM LAWSON)

Maiden of Morven.

(AN OSSIANIC LOVE LAMENT)

MOAN, ye winds that never sleep,
Howl, ye spirits of the deep,
Roar, ye torrents down the steep,
Roll, ye mists on Morven.
May the tempest never rest,
Nor the seas with peace be blest,
Since they tore thee from my breast,
Maiden of Morven!

Fairer than the flowers that grow,
Purer than the rills that flow,
Gentler than the fallow doe
'Mid the woods of Morven;
As the leaf is to the tree,
As the summer to the bee,
So wert thou, my love, to me,
Maiden of Morven!

Ossian's harp sings Fingal's praise ;
Wild the lilt of Carril's lays,
Men and maids of other days
    Fire his tales of Morven ;
Though their chords like thunder roll,
When at Beltane brims the bowl,
Thou'rt the music of my soul
    Maiden of Morven !

Oft I chased the deer of yore ;
Many a battle brunt I bore,
When the chiefs of Innistore
    Hurled their might on Morven.
Blunt my spear and slack my bow,
Like an empty ghost I go,
Death the only hope I know,
    Maiden of Morven !

Skye Boat Song.

(JACOBITE)

S PEED, bonnie boat, like a bird on the wing,
   "Onward," the sailors cry ;
Carry the lad that's born to be king,
  Over the sea to Skye.
     Loud the winds howl, loud the waves roar,
      Thunder-clouds rend the air ;
     Baffled, our foes stand by the shore ;
      Follow, they will not dare.
         Speed, bonnie boat, &c.

Though the waves leap, soft shall ye sleep :
  Ocean's a royal bed ;
Rocked in the deep, Flora will keep
  Watch by your weary head.
         Speed, bonnie boat, &c.

Many's the lad fought on that day
  Well the claymore could wield,
When the night came, silently lay
  Dead on Culloden's field.
          Speed, bonnie boat, &c.

Burned are our homes, exile and death
  Scatter the loyal men ;
Yet ere the sword cool in the sheath,
  Charlie will come again.
          Speed, bonnie boat, &c.

Lament for Maclean of Ardgour.

WAIL loudly, ye women, your coronach doleful,
　　Lament him, ye pipers, tread solemn and slow,
Mown down like a flower is the chief of Ardgour,
And the hearts of the clansmen are weary with woe.
In peace-time he ruled like a father among us,
Unconquered in fight was the blade that he bore,
But the chase was the glory and pride of his manhood,
—Strong Donald the hunter, Macgillian More.

Low down by yon burn that's half hidden with heather
He lurked like a lion in the lair he knew well,
'Twas there sobbed the red deer to feel his keen dagger,
There pierced by his arrow the cailzie-cock fell.
How oft when at e'en he would watch for the wild fowl,
Like lightning his coracle sped from the shore ;
But still, and for aye, as we cross the lone lochan,
Is Donald the hunter, Macgillian More.

Once more let his war-cry resound in the mountains,
Macdonalds shall hear it in eerie Glencoe,
Its echoes shall float o'er the braes of Lochaber,
Till Stewarts at Appin that slogan shall know ;
And borne to the waters beyond the Loch Linnhe,
'Twixt Morven and Mull where the tide-eddies roar,
Macgillians shall hear it and mourn for their kinsman,
For Donald the hunter, Macgillian More.

Then here let him rest in the lap of Scaur Donald,
The wind for his watcher, the mist for his shroud,
Where the green and the grey moss will weave their
    wild tartans,
A covering meet for a chieftain so proud.
For, free as the eagle, these rocks were his eyrie,
And free as the eagle his spirit shall soar
O'er the crags and the corries that erst knew the footfall
Of Donald the hunter, Macgillian More.

SELECTIONS FROM
"SONGS OF THE FOUR NATIONS"
(Music arranged by ARTHUR SOMERVELL)

Pretty Polly Oliver.
(ENGLISH)

OH! Pretty Polly Oliver, the pride of her sex,
　　The love of a grenadier her poor heart did vex;
He courted her so faithful in the good town of Bow,
But marched off to foreign lands a-fighting the foe.

" I cannot rest single nor false I'll not prove,
So I'll list for a drummer-boy and follow my love ;
Peak cap, loopèd jacket, white gaiters and drum,
And marching so manfully to my true love I'll come."

'Twas the battle of Blenheim, in a hot fusilade,
A poor little drummer boy was prisoner made,
But a brave grenadier fought his way thro' the foe,
And fifteen fierce Frenchmen together laid low.

He bore the boy tenderly in his arms as he swooned,
He opened his jacket for to search for a wound ;
"O pretty Polly Oliver, my bravest, my bride,
Your true love shall nevermore be torn from your side."

The birds they sang joyously in that far foreign land,
The drums beat triumphantly with bugle and band ;
Said Marlborough, "Queen Anne and all England shall hear
How I wed Polly Oliver to the brave grenadier."

The Mackintosh's Lament.

(HIGHLAND)

GRIEF of heart! Heart of grief!
Fallen is the warrior chief;
Fallen, like a summer leaf,
Lies Clan Chattan's glory!

Cursed thy breed, thou treacherous steed,
That failed the rider at his need!
Black thy colour, black the deed,
Black thy name in story!

Bitter doom! Hapless bride,
Newly parted from his side,
When my true love stricken sore,
Met his death ill-fated!

Wine for wedding feast prepared,
Friends at wake and funeral shared;
Sorrow, sorrow, evermore!
The bride must mourn unmated.

All Through the Night.
(Welsh)

SLEEP, my love, and peace attend thee,
  All through the night;
Guardian angels God will lend thee
  All through the night;
Soft the drowsy hours are creeping,
Hill and dale in slumber steeping,
Love alone his watch is keeping
  All through the night;

Though I roam, a minstrel lonely,
  All through the night;
My true harp shall praise thee only,
  All through the night;
Love's young dream, alas, is over,
Yet my strains of love shall hover
Near the presence of my lover
  All through the night;

Hark! A solemn bell is ringing
  Clear through the night;
Thou my love art heavenward winging,
  Home through the night;
Earthly dust from off thee shaken,
Soul immortal, thou shalt waken,
With thy last dim journey taken
  Home through the night.

The Castle of Dromore.

(IRISH)

OCTOBER winds lament around the Castle of
   Dromore,
But peace is in her lofty halls, mo páiste veg asthore;
Though autumn leaves may droop and die, a bud of
   spring are you,
Sing hushaby lullaloo lo lan, sing hushaby lullaloo.

Bring no ill-winds to hinder us, my helpless babe
   and me,
Dread spirits of the Blackwater, Clan Eoghan's
   wild banshee;
For Holy Mary, pitying us, in heaven for grace doth
   sue;
Sing hushaby lullaloo lo lan, sing hushaby lullaloo.

Take time to thrive, my rose of hope in the garden
   of Dromore.
Take heed, young eaglet, till your wings have
   feathers fit to soar.
A little rest, and then the world is full of work to do;
Sing hushaby lullaloo lo lan, sing hushaby lullaloo.

The Tree in the Wood;

or, Young Denis.
(IRISH)

✢

OVER the hill young Denis follows the deer,
    Hound, horn, and hunting spear to bring him to
      bay ;
Soaring aloft in heaven the lark carols clear,
    Green waves the leafy wood, for to-morrow's Mayday.
Loud rings his horn all the day from the hill to the sea,
    Faint far away through the wood till the fall of the
      night ;
Weary he rests with his hounds 'neath the hollow oak
      tree,
    Foolish he sinks into sleep by the silver moonlight.

Fairer than mortal rose a maid from the briar,
    Singing a song more sweet than mortal can tell ;
Touched him on brow and lip with kisses of fire,
    Gave him to drink the wine of magical spell.

Swift to the dance of the fairies she bore him away,
  Crowned him her lover, and King of the mad revelry ;
Dead lay his hounds on the sward at the dawn of Mayday,
  Gone was young Denis that slept 'neath the hollow oak
    tree !

Over the hill a horn the forester hears,
  When leaves are waving green and to-morrow's May-
    day ;
Leading the dance at night a maiden appears,
  Linked with a huntsman clad in gallant array.
Masterless now are his cattle that low on the hill,
  Sad his companions that wonder and wait him in vain ;
Bowed in the ashes his mother, that mourns for him still,
  Back to the sunlight young Denis comes never again.

Selections from "*EIGHT VOCAL DUETS*"

(Set to Music by THEO. MARZIALS)

Tears.

TEARS of youth that seem so bitter,
    Dews of sorrow brief,
Are but April drops that glitter
    On the quickening leaf.

Tears there be of other fashion,
    Shed when trees are bare,
Tears of wan and wasted passion,
    Ceaseless in despair.

Tears that burdened hearts deliver,
    When the storm has tossed
Leaf and rain-drop in the river,
    Swept to sea and lost.

Light Vows.

AUTUMN damp and chilly
Shrivels rose and lily.
Sing lullaby for the year.
'Twas but pleasant weather
Held our hearts together ;
And so farewell my dear.

Nay ! No soft denial
Can put back the dial ;
Sing lullaby for the year.
A little frost has blighted
Vows too rashly plighted ;
And so farewell my dear.

Now our dream is shattered,
And the leaves are scattered.
Sing lullaby for the year.
You will go in laughter,
I shall sigh hereafter ;
And so farewell my dear.

MAYTIDE IN MY GARDEN

(A sequence of Six Songs set to Music by Frederic Cowen)

I.

The Coming of May.

WHAT have you brought me, merry Maytide,
    Now that the winter is over?
Trees grown green on the warm hillside,
    Meadows of grass and clover.

White thorn, pink thorn, lilac and lime,
    Cowslip and crowsfoot yellow;
Sunny hours in the long daytime,
    Twilights mild and mellow.

Will you be constant, merry Maytide?
    April was fair but fickle;
Hardly the smile on her face had died,
    Ere the tears would downward trickle.

April is cousin of March the churl,
  With east wind bitterly blowing;
Safely in May will the buds uncurl,
  Ah! May's the time for growing!

May brings wealth to my garden trim,
  Song-birds in bush and bower,
With the brown bee humming a wedding hymn,
  And marrying flower to flower.

II.

Voices in the Garden.

I HEAR glad notes in the garden,
  Ringing from tree to tree,
Voices of wandering minstrels
  That sojourn awhile with me.

They build in the hawthorn hedgerow,
  And under the laurel leaves;
I thank them for choosing my garden,
  And twittering 'neath my eaves.

III.

Morning Flow'rets.

❀

M ORNING flowerets drenched with dew
Have not fresher looks than you,
Have not fairer form.

Dainty crest and slender stem
You can show to rival them,
Colour soft and warm.

They, poor things, will wither soon,
Creatures of an afternoon,
Pretty toys at best.

Let them wither! You shall bide
In my garden at my side,
Sweetest, loveliest!

IV.

Mayday and Maynight.

A BRIGHT Mayday is Queen of the year,
   In Nature's kingdom she owns no peer,
The flowers in blossom, the birds in tune,
The whole earth radiant in golden noon.

No, no! Maynight is balmiest, best,
When all but angels and lovers rest;
—Fond lovers! How oft to her arms they repair,
And whisper their secrets securely there.

V.

Falling Blossoms.

I T cannot be you die outright
  Dear blooms of May,
That fall on the pathway pink and white,
  Or float on the wind away;

You are but lent to bless our earth awhile,
Then turned to twinkling stars from Heaven you smile.

VI.

Elegy.

MAY-MONTH is dying, few are her hours ;
   Oh ! But the days went so cheerily ;
June heat will wither her delicate flowers.
   Toll the bell, toll the bell drearily.

Summer is with us, but Spring left behind ;
   Oh ! But the days went so cheerily.
Her faltering farewell is heard in the wind.
   Toll the bell, toll the bell drearily.

Gone is her freshness, her glory, her spell ;
   Oh ! But the days went so cheerily ;
Toll from your belfry, each little blue-bell.
   Toll the bell, toll the bell drearily.

SELECTIONS FROM "TWELVE SONGS"
(Set to Music by THEO. MARZIALS)

The Voice of the Wind.

I HEARD the voice of the wind
 Telling a happy tale,
In a land where summer is kind
And the roses never fail.

It chanted of faith sublime,
 Of young love trustful and true,
Of strong wings eager to climb
 To heavens of boundless blue.

I heard the voice of the wind
 Moaning a lilt of grief,
Of hope left halting behind,
 Of darkness and dead belief.

Then it sighed as tho' it would cease,
 With a softer, kindlier breath,
For it whispered a song of peace,
 And the name of that song was death.

None the Less.

"YES" was a yoeman six-foot high,
    Leaning on his garden rail ;
"No" was a little maid slim and shy,
    Hurrying home with a milking pail.
"Yes" said "Come by the wicket gate,
    I'll help carry your pail, Oh ! come ;"
"No" was sorry but "No" was late,
    And "No" must now be hurrying home :
"No" said "No," but "Yes" said "Yes"
    And "No" was lingering none the less.

"Yes" had a garden of roses red,
    "No" was sweet in a neat white gown ;
Sweets to the sweet, sweetheart "Yes" said,
    "No" but made him a shy little frown.
"Here's a great full-blown rose, that's me.
    Here's a little pink bud, that's you.
Wear them there for company,
    For both alike in my garden grew."
"No" said "No," but "Yes" said "Yes"
    And "No" is wearing them none the less.

"Yes" had wonderful news to tell,
  "No" had never the time to hear;
Yet "Yes" kept her till twilight fell,
  Ten times over to tell it clear.
Sweet the little stars peep'd on high,
  Sweet the night wind stirred the wood,
Sweet the nightingale piped hard by,
  And "No" made answer fair and good.
And "No" said "No," but "No" means "Yes"
  When maids are wooed and won, I guess;
For "Yes" will marry her none the less.

The Rosebud.

A ROSEBUD lay a-sleeping,
    As pure as April dew,
Her dreams were in God's keeping,
    No earthly thought she knew.

But a south wind warm and tender
    Unsealed her petals fair ;
She flushed into crimson splendour
    Her heart of hearts lay bare.

And first for joy she started,
    And then she sighed in pain
For the rosebud days departed,
    Never to come again.

A Song of Gladness.

EARTH'S rich bosom hath many a blossom,
  Fair, fair is she clad ;
Regal splendour the sun doth lend her,
  Sing, sing and be glad.

Pipe your loudest and look your proudest,
  Blithe birds while ye may ;
Summer glories are short-lived stories,
  Brief, brief is their day.

Earthly Maytime and earthly playtime
  Soon, soon will be past,
When our Father his own shall gather
  Home, home at the last.

Love will Endure.

(Set to Music by ALFRED SCOTT-GATTY)

I BUILT my dear a summer nest
   Pavilioned o'er with leafy boughs,
Where woodland flowers are loveliest,
   And a quiet river flows.
There in a bower of beauty bright,
   Our bliss was sweet and sure,
Our song a burden of delight,
   "Love will endure."
        Be not afraid,
           True heart and pure;
        Though all else fade,
           Love will endure.

I made my dear a winter bed
   Out on the lonely cold hillside;
The snow falls lightly at her head,
   And all the flowers have died.
Her sentries are the cypresses,
   That guard her sleep secure,
Her dirge is whispered on the breeze,
   —"Love will endure."
        Rest, rest in peace,
           True heart and pure;
        Tho' hope may cease,
           Love will endure.

Gillian.

(Set to Music by Charles Bethune)

I SAW you passing, Gillian,
  Under my window wide;
And twenty steps have brought me
  To your side.

Here in the old rose garden
  I love to see you best,
For all the world a rose-bud
  Like the rest.

And will you scold me, Gillian?
  And have I done amiss,
To dye your roses redder
  With a kiss?

"Thoughts of You."

Translated from the French of François Coppée.

(Set to Music by TIVADAR NACHEZ)

❦

WHEN I behold a pure white rose
    Open 'neath skies of summer blue,
Ever my heart more heavy grows:
    'Tis that it makes me dream of you,
        When I behold a rose.

When I behold the evening star,
    Why must I check the rising tear?
'Tis that your eyes as radiant are,
    And I would fain that you were near,
        When I behold a star.

When autumn swallows southward fly,
    Vanished till April comes anew,
Why does my heart within me die?
    'Tis that I'm exiled far from you,
        When swallows southward fly.

Irish Spinning Song.

(Arranged by ARTHUR SOMERVELL)

1st voice.   O WHERE have you been my pretty Kathleen,
          When the day was first beginnin'?
2nd voice. I wandered down to the Lis so green
          To gather the flax for the spinnin'.

Chorus.
With a tow row row and a tow row row,
    We're handy girls at spinnin';
'Tis we know how to spin the thread
    Will weave the snow-white linen.

1st voice.   And who have you seen my pretty Kathleen?
          'Twas neither brother nor father.
2nd voice. Small wonder then with a world full of men
          If it had been someone I'd rather.

Chorus—With a tow row row, &c.

1st voice.   Was it Shamus O'Neil, was it Rory O'More?
               Was it Patrick or Dermot Daly?
2nd voice.   No name was pinned on his coathamore
               Or printed upon his shillaleagh.

               Chorus—With a tow row row, &c.

1st voice.   Suppose it was Dermot ye parted from late
               With his poll so crisp and curly?
2nd voice.   There'd be Carolan's receipt for the whisky neat,
               And a wedding in the Shrovetide early.

               Chorus—With a tow row row, &c.

Love the Harvester.

(Set to Music by ALFRED CELLIER)

ONE autumn evening straying,
    My listless feet were borne
Where Love grown tired of playing
    Was harvesting his corn.

And hearts both true and fickle
    Within his sheaf he bound,
As, with his silver sickle,
    He wandered o'er the ground.

But straggling hither, thither,
    Such wanton ways he had,
Good ears he'd leave to wither
    And gather in the bad.

Then did I scold him soundly
    For what I witnessed there,
And rated him most roundly,
    This sorry harvester.

Love laughed till in each dimple
    A tear of mirth did fall.
"My statute book is simple
    I know no laws at all!"

DATE DUE

LIBRARY
UNIVERSITY OF CALIFORNIA
RIVERSIDE

Ex Libris
ISAAC FOOT

SONGS UNSUNG.

Songs

Sung and Unsung

BY

HAROLD BOULTON.

LONDON:
The Leadenhall Prefs, Ltd : 50, Leadenhall Street, E.C.
Simpkin, Marshall, Hamilton, Kent & Co., Ltd :

New York : Charles Scribner's Sons, 743 & 745, Broadway.

THE LEADENHALL PRESS, LTD:
50, LEADENHALL STREET, LONDON, E.C.
T 4,652.

Preface to Songs Unsung.

THE idea that poems intended for singing are necessarily unreadable for their own sake is too bad a compliment to music to be tolerated — at all events by the poet. Words suitable for musical setting must obey certain canons both of form and matter, a fact well known to writer and composer. It need not follow that their inception is the less spontaneous nor their rank in the realm of literature the less dignified, since every branch of art has its own limitations.

Such sympathetic care has been bestowed by musicians on former words of his, that the writer of the present collection is inclined to hope that a similarly happy fate will befal these also.

Accordingly, four score and four new songs are here sent out into the world to take their chance with whatever graces and imperfections they may contain.

H. B.

INDEX.

SONGS UNSUNG.

	PAGE.
A little time, a little love	11
Amo, I love thee, dear	12
A lovely briar rose I had	13
Apple blossoms pink and white	15
Ah! come with me into the fairyland	16
At midnight as I slumbered	17
A magpie gossiped to his mate	18
As I went out to the wood	20
Beyond the dim horizon rim	22
Climbing the clouds of golden light	24
Down in the alley of chestnuts	26
Fresh dewdrops from the font of night	27
Fly not away, my childhood's dreams	28
High in the valley ere the March was done	29
Have a care mariner how you go!	31
How shall I win my lady's pleasure?	33
Hope was a flower at the dawn of day	34
Huntsman, what cheer?	35
If I were Love	37
I saw a ship come sailing	38
If you but deign your favour	39
It was a wandering star had strayed	40

	PAGE
In winter when the world is numb	41
I go when I dream to a valley of flowers	42
I looked across the stream	43
In cavern cool the mermaid bides	45
I saw two lovers wend their way	46
I lost my ladylove, I know not how	47
I'd love some drowsy summer noon	48
In the waning of our daytime	49
Love is my complement, my all in all	50
Midnight, and not a cloud to dim	51
My thoughts took wing to a merry greenwood	52
No ripple stirs the pearly lake	53
Near my heart with face half hidden	54
Now sheet and blanket, children dear	55
O gondola with silver prow	56
Out on the moor I think of you	58
O red-rose lips I loved to kiss	59
On the lakes of Killarney	60
O'er seas of blue I haste to you	61
O purest pearl of Paradise	62
Our orchards wear a mantle white	63
O blest above all roses	64
One little word I ask of thee	65
Pink buds upon the cherry	66
Smitten with frost and snow	67
Swiftly our boat has borne us down with the stream	68
Song of the mavis	69
Sleep little soldiers of Christ the King	70
Some sing their song of woman's love	71
The evening wind blows cool in the wheat	73
The summer days are gone for aye	74
The water springs so cool and clear	75
Throughout the fragrant summer night	76

ix.

	PAGE.
The first red rose of summer is here	77
Tell me, where is the fortunate isle	78
The shivering bird is silent	79
There are four pretty maids live down at the mill	80
The dew in the morn	81
The sun sinks lower	82
The snow falls, not a wind doth sigh	83
The nightingale has taken flight	84
The first leaf has fallen	85
The worst of the winter is over	86
The leaves are lightly shaken	87
The seed a bird let fall	88
'Twas heedless happy April-tide	89
The false love that I loved so well	90
Up in merry treeland yonder	91
Within my heart is a palace	92
Where can a maid a true love find?	93
Wild flowers of folly springing where we walk	94
Will you come sailing on yonder cloud	95
What thoughts the budding year brings in	96
Would you, old earth again	97
When winter leaves the frozen north	98
When the logs were burning bright	99
When winter seas are drear and dun	100
When hill and dale look merriest in May	101
When fairies through the flowers flit	102
Yon leaf again we shall not see	103
You came like a vision bright	104
Well! Good night, all! Our songs are sung	105

A Little Time.

A LITTLE time, a little love,
    When youthful hearts beat high;
A gathered flower, a treasured glove,
    A smile, a sigh.

A spring-tide of fond fellowship,
    'Mid quickening bud and blade;
A traffic sweet of hand and lip,
    In woodland shade.

A parting of two lives that fear
    No tempest from the shore,
Trustful of joys to reappear,
    That come no more.

Wild tears of hope deferred, denied,
    Where winter storms contend.
White flowers upon a lone graveside,
    And so the end.

The Latin Lesson.

AMO, I love thee, dear,
   Amas, thou lovest me ;
And how we learn love's lesson here
   No jealous eye can see.
Amamus, and of that
   The world is ignorant ;
Amo, Amas, Amat,
   Amamus, Amatis, Amant.

Amabam, I loved thee
   Since first I saw thy face,
Amabas, thou by slow degree
   Did'st take me into grace.
Amabamus, we've sat,
   And laughed at care and cant ;
Amo, Amas, Amat,
   Amamus, Amatis, Amant.

Amabo, I'll love thee
   In future as in past ;
Amabis, thou'lt be true to me
   While Love and Latin last.
Amabimus, Oh ! What,
   What more can lovers want ?
Amo, Amas, Amat,
   Amamus, Amatis, Amant.

The Briar Rose.

A LOVELY briar rose I had
    Within my garden fair ;
Its budding glory made me glad
    To see it growing there.

I tended it most lovingly
    From bud to blossom tide,
The treasure of my heart to be,
    My comfort and my pride.

But open stood my garden gate,
    I tarried otherwhere,
Mine enemy, that lay in wait,
    Despoiled my rose-tree fair.

She shed her fragrance round his head,
    Her petals at his feet,
Her stem was bruised, her bloom was fled,
    —My rose that was so sweet.

In passion at my wasted toil
　I played a madman's part,
I tore her roots from out the soil,
　Her image from my heart.

But a passing wind in pity bore
　New seed to the broken ground,
And where my briar bloomed before
　Behold! Heartsease I found.

The Fortune Teller's Song.

APPLE blossoms pink and white
Clothe the orchard with delight;
    Bless you pretty lady.
Flowers upon the ground that grow
No such tender colours know,
Daintier still your face doth show,
    Doubt not pretty lady.
    Hey no, nonino,
    Hey no, nonino,
    Hey no, nonino,
        Ho Heigho!

Apple fruit is gold and red,
When the summer time is sped,
    Bless you pretty lady.
Pluck the blossom from the tree,
Who will then the apple see?
Pray your fortune better be,
    Farewell pretty lady.
    Hey no, nonino,
    Hey no, nonino,
    Hey no, nonino,
        Ho Heigho!

The Fairyland.

AH! come with me into the fairyland,
　　That lovers, if they will, may find,
Where Hope's bright palaces unshaken stand
　　And hearts are ever true and kind.
　　　　There are new-world treasures,
　　　　And new-world pleasures,
With the old-world trouble left behind.

There's laughter and dancing to a merry tune,
　　On a green lawn bordered by the deep ;
There's a murmur of music in the afternoon
　　From flutes that summon you to sleep,
　　　　Blown fainter and slower
　　　　As the sun dips lower,
And silent when the small stars peep.

And if you'll follow it for love's sweet sake,
　　The way lies readily at hand,
There's a door to open and a spell to break,
　　'Tis you have the key at your command ;
　　　　Let the word be spoken,
　　　　Let the spell be broken,
And we'll step into that fairyland.

A Dream.

AT midnight as I slumbered,
    Great heart-content I knew,
The beat of wings unnumbered,
Anear my pillow drew.

On every snow-white feather
    A light etherial glowed,
Sweet voices blent together
    In rhythmic concord flowed.

But all the heavenly faces
    That starlike hover there,
The dawning daylight chases
    Save one, the fairest fair!

O kindly Cupid hear me,
    And grant this boon divine,
To dream the maiden near me,
    And wake to find her mine!

The Magpies.

A MAGPIE gossiped to his mate
    Out of an old beech tree,
"There is no songster small or great
    Can pipe like you and me."

"In sooth," replied his consort pied,
    "I think the self-same thing;
So rare a note was ne'er afloat
    Since music first found wing.

"Sad nightingale we must taboo,
    That mourns unto the moon;
How dully drones the poor cuckoo,
    How often out of tune!

"To be the giddy lark I'd blush
    That high in heaven doth mount,
The dove, the blackbird and the thrush,
    I hold of no account.

"But the finest music in the grove,
  What e'er the fashion be,
Is when I chatter and chirp to my love,
  And you chatter and chirp to me."

So then in fond abandonment
  They sang their song again.
—God grant us all to be content,
  As were those magpies twain.

Song with Refrain in Chorus for Girls.

A S I went out to the wood,
   Where the sweet birds call,
A stag beside me stood ;
   Dance merrily maidens all.
His horns were branched like the tall oak tree,
And his eyes on mine looked tenderly,
As he lightly tripped o'er the turf to me,
   Dance merrily maidens all.
His head so proud on my arm was laid,
By dell and dale we gently strayed
Where the moss is green in the forest glade,
   And the sweet birds call.

The lusty horns rang out,
   Dance merrily maidens all ;
Loud loud the huntsmen's shout,
   Where the sweet birds call ;
Away to the hills my loved one flew,
And laughed as his light feet brushed the dew,
Till the wearied huntsmen homeward drew,
   Dance merrily maidens all.

I found my love far over the hill,
When the sun was low and the wood was still,
By cooling streams we sipped our fill,
    Where the sweet birds call.

    Summer and song are good,
      Dance merrily maidens all,
    'Tis fine to walk in the wood,
      Where the sweet birds call.

Dreamland.

BEYOND the dim horizon rim
    Behind the twilight hills,
Where radiant air beyond compare
    The windless valley fills,
'Mid music of immortal streams
Is the country of our dreams.

There enters nought of evil thought
    Within these pastures pure ;
Caves grim and steep in the hills of sleep
    All fearful dreams immure ;
Here only visions glorified
And hallowed memories bide.

Here laugh, amid white lilies hid,
    The baby dreamers blest,
And mothers smile to press awhile
    Lost darlings to their breast ;
Here youths, with raptured fancy thrilled,
Hope's airy fabrics build.

All in a glade of myrtle shade,
   Where crystal fountains rain,
True lovers meet in converse sweet
   Whom death had torn in twain,
And taste the bliss that might have been,
In ecstacy serene.

And every breast that craves for rest
   May free its fettered soul,
To roam a space in this fair place,
   And deem its wounds are whole ;
Then wake to earth's dull task anew
Refreshed with heavenly dew.

A Woman's Soul.

CLIMBING the clouds of golden light
　　To the infinite azure plain,
The soul of a woman winged its flight,
　　Set free from its mortal chain.

Cold and clear was the day that shone
　　In that silent solitude ;
And shivering, trembling, all alone,
　　The spirit uncertain stood.

The time-worn world looked warm and red
　　In the gleam of the rising sun,
Above was many a sphere to tread
　　Ere the gates of heaven were won.

Sadly the wanderer gazed below
　　On an earthly dwelling place,
Where a strong man wept by a bed of woe
　　And bent o'er a lifeless face.

Then rang the voices of Seraphim
From the uttermost Heaven above,
" Daughter thine unnamed prayers for him
Are won by thine unsoiled love ;

" Comfort thyself, who art sore distressed
For the soul thou fain would'st free ;
For when thou findest the Father's rest
That other shall be with thee."

The Alley of Chestnuts.

DOWN in the alley of chestnuts
    Little child Marjorie cries,
All for a toy that is broken,
    Drowning her bright blue eyes ;
But when the clouds are blackest,
    Lubin comes up behind,
Soothes her with boyish caresses,
    Kisses, and comforts kind.

Down in the alley of chestnuts
    Many a year's gone by ;
All for the love of a maiden
    Lubin must sit and sigh ;
But when the clouds are blackest
    Draws maid Marjorie near,
Says to the heart that is breaking
    Words that are life to hear.

Now is the alley of chestnuts
    Brimming with love and joy ;
No more sighs for a lover,
    Nor tears for a broken toy.
The toys and the hearts that are brittle
    Darken the world with woe ;
The charm that has magic to mend them
    Lubin and Marjorie know.

Eternal Spring.

FRESH dewdrops from the font of night
    The new-born Maybuds christen,
And feather-coated choirs invite
    The wakening world to listen.

Thro' all the woodland aisles they wing,
    As did their sires before them;
And while their old-world hymns they sing
    New-fangled folks adore them.

The green young year they celebrate,
    The home-returning swallow,
Spring blossoms pale and delicate,
    With summer flowers to follow.

All nature feels this nameless spell
    That wintry care assuages,
Men's hearts fly up to heaven as well,
    Like birds set free from cages.

So welcome gracious spring appears!
    Its glamour tires us never;
It hath been so ten thousand years,
    And will be so for ever.

Fly Not Away.

FLY not away, my childhood's dreams,
   To light my path your sunlight bring,
Your music shed on woods and streams
   Your nameless charm on everything.

Ye golden hours, your chariot stay
   That hastes across the hills of time ;
Your eager steeds that spurn delay
   Too soon the steep meridian climb.

Come back, my first and fondest love,
   Too brief a bliss the fates allow ;
I swear by heaven's blue vault above
   I cannot live without thee now.

An Alpine Song.

HIGH in the valley ere the March was done,
    A young south wind came singing ;
He danced in the glory of the golden sun,
    And set the little snowbells ringing ;
For they knew the tale he had come to tell,
So they all rang merrily ding dong dell,
Ding ding a dong ding dong dell.

"Dear little snowbells, the spring is come,
    Set free from its frost-bound prison,
But all other flowers are dead and dumb,
    You only from slumber have risen.
And each of you tinkles her tiny bell,
To ring in the spring with a ding dong dell,
Ding ding a dong ding dong dell.

"The wise old mountains with their heads so hoar
    Will yield to the spring with wonder,
As the torrent and the avalanche, chained no more,
    Leap down with a crash of thunder ;
While I shake you gently and peal the bell
In each little belfry, ding dong dell,
Ding ding a dong ding dong dell.

"But alas! when the river of melted snows
  Makes the grass grow green around you,
Your beauty will wither, and the Alpine rose
  Blush red in the nook where I found you.
I shall sigh as I ring your knell, snowbell,
Ring ding a dong ding, farewell;
Ring ding a dong ding dong dell."

Sea-Scraps.

I.

HAVE a care mariner how you go!
　　There's many a mermaid down below,
Who would woo you there in a palace fair,
And where you had vanished none would know,
Have a care mariner how you go!

****

II.

Wind from the west, wave of the sea,
Waft the ship homeward safely to me;
Rock-reef wound her not, storm forbear,
Convoys of angels keep weather fair.

****

III.

Now fold your wings my faithful barque,
　　And rock yourself to slumber,
That brought my love through tempest dark,
　　Through perils none can number.

Then dream you sail secure from ill,
  On an ocean crystal-paven,
With a happy voyage whenever you will,
  Whenever you will a haven.

You brought my love through tempest dark,
  Through perils none can number,
So fold your wings my faithful barque,
  And rock yourself to slumber.

My Lady's Pleasure.

HOW shall I win my lady's pleasure,
    The one good gift that life can give?
For unpossessed of that fair treasure
    I would not live.

How shall my longing be requited?
    My tongue hath little skill to speak;
Words by most cunning pen indited
    Were far too weak.

Boldly I'll trust my cause unto my lyre,
    And plead, in suppliant wise,
Prayers that sweet music shall inspire
    Toward her to rise.

Go then my song on soaring pinion,
    Such charm of love to her impart,
That at the last thou gain dominion
    Within her heart!

Youth and Hope.

HOPE was a flower at the dawn of day,
    Growing in a sheltered nook ;
Youth was a student, careless, gay,
    Fingering an unread book.

Youth thought the flower was good to pluck,
    Took it for his own ; why not ?
Kissed it, laid it in the leaves for luck,
    Turned the page and forgot.

Long years afterwards Age came there
    At the solemn evening hour ;
The pages he knew by heart lay bare,
    Inside was the withered flower.

Then age, like summer-falling rain,
    Such tears of joy did weep,
That he saw hope's flower bloom fresh again
    Ere he fell for ever asleep.

Old English Hunting Song.

(FOR PART MUSIC)

HUNTSMAN, what cheer?
  Woe betide the deer;
The merry chase comes on apace,
The lusty hounds draw near;
He is swift, he is strong,
And the chase will be long,
But we'll have him at last, never fear.

Huntsman, what cheer?
  Woe betide the deer;
Upleaps the sun to see the run,
At call of chanticleer.
And we'll show him a sight
He shall hail with delight,
Ere the top of the morning be here.

Huntsman, what cheer?
  Woe, alack, the deer;
  His race is run, the chase is done,
  Yon hurdle is his bier;
  And the feast shall be spread,
  And the grace be said
When the stars in the welkin appear.

   The Grace.
        With no ill will
        Our meat we kill,
        But all with good intent;
        So may God's benison
        On this good venison
        And all true men be sent.

If I were Love.

If I were Love,
How many ways to mortal mind
My power I'd prove ;
I'd prove it clear and wise and kind,
Not as men's slander paints it—blind !

Each fault or flaw
In fickle hearts a kiss should mend,
That should be law ;
Light heart true wounded heart should tend,
Thus every pretty tale should end.

I should decree
Men goodly all, maids lily-fair ;
For both I'd see
A fitting mate, someday, somewhere,
But age should have no portion there.

And as for you,
Sweetheart, unfettered, wayward, light !
This much I'd do—
Such troth your lips should plead and plight,
Our life would be one long delight.
Ah me ! How wise I'd prove,
If I were Love !

The Dream Ship.

I SAW a ship come sailing,
　　Come sailing o'er the sea,
With mariners all crimson clad
　　That seemed to beckon me.
There was no ripple on the wave,
　　There was no wind astir,
But silently the vessel drave
　　On wings of gossamer;
The masts of silver and of gold
　　Across the water gleamed,
　　—Thus was it that I dreamed.

The deck was filled with flowers,
　　The hum of bees was heard,
Each mast became a myrtle tree
　　Alive with many a bird;
And some, like leaves in autumn-tide,
　　Flew rustling thro' the air,
But one that fluttered to my side
　　Sang wondrous fondly there;
And to the lilt of that fond lay
　　My heart the answer seemed.
　　—I could not think I dreamed.

My Song.

IF you but deign your favour,
  Unto the song I sing,
Such lilt of love I'll fashion
That echoes of compassion
Within your heart shall ring ;
If you but deign your favour,
To hear the song I sing.

Then Love, emplanted newly
By virtue of my song,
In sunshine of your bosom
Shall grow from bud to blossom
With increase sure and strong,
Till you shall love me truly,
As I have loved you long.

BALLAD.

A Wandering Star.

IT was a wandering star had strayed
   From the bright ethereal plain ;
     Her hand she laid
On the utmost gate of heaven's domain,
   And found the gate ajar.
Out on the dizzy brink she crept
   And careless slept,
And fell into our mortal sphere
   And woke and wept.
Poor lonely wandering star !

E'en now her glorious home she minds
   In desolate distress ;
     Nor comfort finds,
For stains of earth's unloveliness
   Her heavenly lustre mar.
Full wearied of her wanderings,
   She beats vain wings
Against her prison barrier drear,
   And sobs and sings.
Poor lonely fallen star !

Song of the Seasons.

IN winter when the world is numb,
   I keep a cheery heart,
Because I know that spring will come,
   When winter doth depart.

When spring and summer reign supreme,
   I'm thankful with the rest,
And autumn, like a golden dream,
   Sits lightly on my breast.

When winter doth again appear,
   I greet him as a friend,
For I know he brings me every year
   Nearer my journey's end.

The Valley of Flowers.

I GO when I dream to a valley of flowers,
   My home ere I woke in this hard world of ours;
It is set like a gem mid the mountains of snow,
But mild as the May are the breezes that blow.

No need of the sun and the moon to give light,
A glimmering star is each blossom of white;
For each is a spirit immortal and blest,
Unborn on the earth, or come home to its rest.

But where lies that valley no mortal may tell,
Though pure hearts of children remember it well;
And thither in sleep may the weary take wing,
And the swallows wait there for the coming of spring.

There is one gone before whom in dreaming I call,
Whom I seek where the lilies are brightest of all;
How short is the time, but how heavy the hours,
Till we stand side by side in the valley of flowers.

Whispers.

I LOOKED across the stream
　In flickering moonlight gleam,
And the beauty of the night
But saddened me ;

Lonely and tempest-tossed,
My thoughts their peace had lost,
And jarred in strange despite,
Discordantly.

I heard a whisper soft
From out the apple croft,
I deemed it was the breeze
Among the trees.

And yet my heart's unrest
Some healing balm confessed,
Some presence nearer drew
Ere yet I knew.

Two hands were in my own,
My heart, tumultuous grown,
Scarce knew itself aright
The joy it bore.

I looked in two dear eyes
Tender as moonlit skies,
And found my heart's delight
For evermore.

The Mermaid.

IN cavern cool the mermaid bides
    Beyond the pulse of restless tides,
Where angry storms are not ;
Nor winter cold nor summer heat
Against her pearly palace beat,
In coral bowers she weaves sea-flowers,
And wails her loveless lot.

The sailor sinks with scarce a sob,
The stars above him reel and throb,
The storm's a far off drone ;
Over his soul the great seas surge,
Like silver bells he hears his dirge,
He hears her croon a dreamy tune,
" Be mine alone, alone ! "

Two Lovers.

I SAW two lovers wend their way
   'Mid summer woodlands fair ;
The land in nooontide slumber lay,
   And those two walked in silence there.

Till suddenly some word he spoke
   That made her blush and smile,
And waves of rippling laughter woke
   The drowsy air that dreamed erewhile.

A soft wind roused the trees from sleep,
   Up roused the birds as well,
The rill that tumbled down the steep
   Made crystal music as it fell.

And all the voices seemed to say
   " The world is just begun,
" For love is newborn every day
   "And love and harmony are one."

My Lost Ladylove.

I LOST my ladylove, I know not how,
   And sought her diligently low and high ;
But have no care to find her now,
   I know not why.

Perchance her waywardness my patience wore,
   For oft in vain I courted her unkind ;
And finding favour, found no more
   Content of mind.

Some other where she plagues some other one,
   Deigning his peace and quiet to destroy ;
Then since he seeks what now I shun,
   —I wish him joy !

Drifting.

I'D love some drowsy summer noon
    To launch our shallop from the shore,
And creep along with lazy oar
Across the silent calm lagoon.

Or we would hoist an idle sail
That hardly flapped against the mast,
And haply drift to sea at last,
Before the ebbing tide should fail.

Let leagues of sea from home divide,
Or chance our shallop homeward bear ;
I would not ask nor think nor care,
So you were ever by my side.

Memories.

IN the waning of our daytime,
　　Surely, Love, our life is fair,
Radiant still with hues of Maytime,
　　Ringing still with music rare.
Olden melodies, golden memories,
　　Ghosts of the years gone by,
Float before us in shadowy chorus,
　　Bright with the love that can never die.

What though leaf and grape may vanish,
　　And the vine be stripped and bare?
Love hath vintage left to banish
　　Winter cold and winter care.
Olden melodies, golden memories,
　　Ghosts of the years gone by,
All are stories of long-lost glories,
　　All but the love that can never die.

True heart, now the light is dimmer,
　　And the sands of time run low,
Let us look beyond the glimmer
　　Of the twilight after-glow ;
Olden melodies, golden memories,
　　Ghosts of the years gone by,
Swift as swallow, we long to follow
　　Over the sea where the soft winds sigh,
Where the dreams of the past find a haven at last,
　　And love and summer can never die.

Love's Completeness.

L OVE is my complement, my all in all,
　Wherewith considered all things else wax small.

If I be rich without Love, poor am I;
If I be poor, Love fills my treasury.
It is my sword against the world to wage,
My shield of shelter from ill fortune's rage.

Love is my song, my solace and my joy,
My honey-food that nevermore doth cloy;
Through life till death my comrade bides it still,
And after that I hope in heaven it will.

I find no cause to vex, whate'er befall,
With Love my complement, my all in all.

"Midnight."
(AN ODE WITHOUT AN S.)

MIDNIGHT, and not a cloud to dim
　　The radiant mirror of the moon,
　　　　Upon the deep below;
The heaven all clear from rim to rim
Doth counterfeit the blue of noon,
　　　　And not a breath doth blow.

Mark yonder meteor in mid air
Dart like an arrow of liquid light
　　　　Athwart the heavenly plain!
'Twill fade and fall we know not where,
To find beyond the realm of night
　　　　Immortal calm again.

And we who look and wonder, know
Our life will but a moment bide
　　　　Within the firmament;
For meteor-like we come and go,
With hope eternal glorified,
　　　　On unknown goal intent.

My Thoughts.

MY thoughts took wing to a merry greenwood,
    All summer and song and mirth ;
But a frosty wind came shivering by,
    And scattered the leaves to earth.

My thoughts went sailing far to sea,
    Where the waves and the sunset meet ;
But a great wave carried them back again,
    And flung them ashore at my feet.

My thoughts lay lost in two bright eyes,
    So honest and brave and true,
That I there found comfort and love enough
    To follow the wide world through.

Boat Song.

NO ripple stirs the pearly lake,
    And idly dips the oar ;
A thousand flowers sweet fragrance make,
    And waft it from the shore.
Serenely chimes the evening bell
    This balmy night of June,
To bid the golden sun farewell,
    And greet the silver moon.
        O bounteous summer weather,
          O voyage of delight,
        When voices blend together,
          And hearts are tuned aright !

Far up the mountains in the west
    The lengthening shadows creep,
The rosy clouds that light their crest
    Will soon be lulled to sleep.
Sing softly, for repose has come
    To cloud and lake and hill,
No more the nightingale is dumb
    But all things else are still.
        O night of joy and glory,
          O happy evensong,
        When Love 's the lilt and story,
          And Youth is brave and strong !

First Love.

N EAR my heart with face half hidden,
    First-love crept and nestled low;
Though he came a guest unbidden,
    Yet I could not bid him go.
Sighing softly, singing sweetly,
    Soon he won a willing thrall;
Now he holds my heart completely,
    Love to me is all in all.

When at eve the flowers are dreaming,
    And the stars awake above,
Out of heaven their kind eyes beaming,
    Lead me to the one I love.
Worldly wealth let misers measure,
    Worldly fame is mean and small;
Chiefest joy and goodliest treasure,
    Love to me is all in all.

Evening Song for Children.

NOW sheet and blanket, children dear,
    Your tired limbs cover ;
Above your pillows angels peer,
    And round you hover.
In white-winged squadrons from the skies
    They troop at even,
To bring you lilts and lullabies
    From heaven.

We old ones, dulled by worldly rush
    Of toil and traffic,
No longer hear amid the hush
    Their songs seraphic ;
Bnt nestling 'neath their guardian wing
    You slumber purely.
They are the army of the King,
    Most surely !

My Gondola.

O GONDOLA with silver prow,
  That glistens 'neath the moon,
Blest be the tree in every bough
  From which thy form was hewn ;
Swiftly I bid thee bear me now
  O'er yonder calm lagoon.
    Aië! Aië! We deftly steer
      Round palace, pier and quay ;
    Stalì! The waterway grows clear,
      The path is ours. Stalì!

The Sandolo, Burano's boast,
  Falls far behind thy pace ;
Barchette from Fusina's coast
  Dare never give thee chase ;
I'll pledge thy toast before a host
  To sail or row a race.
    Aië! Aië! We deftly steer
      Round palace, pier and quay,
    Stalì! The waterway grows clear,
      The path is ours. Stalì!

O gondola! This night my bride
　Sets forth aboard of thee ;
Round Lido's isle we'll boldly glide,
　And greet the ocean free ;
For love is mighty as the tide,
　And deathless as the sea.
　　　　Aië! Aië! We deftly steer
　　　　　Round palace, pier and quay,
　　　　Stalì! The waterway grows clear,
　　　　　The path is ours.　Stalì!

Out on the Moor.

OUT on the moor I think of you,
    And feel your presence near,
Where the wail of the wind and the wild curlew
    Are the only sounds I hear.

Their voices whisper your name to me,
    From many a mile away;
"Can true love still a truant be?
    Come back, come back," they say.

And come I will, whate'er betide,
    To the love that calls me home;
Finding my peace where you abide,
    —Never again to roam.

A Dirge.

O RED-ROSE lips I loved to kiss,
   O hands so lily-white,
And has our loving come to this,
   That we must part to-night?
     O wearily, wearily,
     Toll the bell drearily,
       For we must part to-night.

O tenderness to sorrow turned
   That nothing can requite,
Have fires that once so fiercely burned
   For ever lost their light?
     O wearily, wearily,
     Toll the bell drearily,
       For love is dead to-night.

Irish Song.

O N the lakes of Killarney
    The storm gathers high,
The shrill winds of winter
    Thro' the bare sallows* cry ;
But wilder my tears are
    Than the storm-driven rain,
Since the truest of lovers
    Comes never again.

If poverty part us,
    Thrice cruel the theft
That stole from my bosom
    The one treasure left ;
I am wasted with watching,
    With waiting in vain,
And 'tis kind death I pray for
    If you come not again.

---

* From the wood of the sallow tree the harps used to be made.

O'er Seas of Blue.

O'ER seas of blue I haste to you,
    My journey's hope and end,
And every gale that fills the sail
    I welcome as a friend.

I see you stand beside the strand,
    Your eyes look out to sea ;
I almost hear the greeting dear
    Your lips will frame for me.

The time draws near, there's nought to fear
    From freak of wind or weather,
Nor wait we long for that glad song
    Our hearts will sing together.

To a Fair Young Soul.

O PUREST pearl of Paradise,
  Set in a mortal setting,
Why dwell you here 'neath earthly skies,
  Your heavenly home forgetting?

How blest the few brief years you stay,
  The parting hour, how grievous!
For you will yearn for home one day,
  And take white wings and leave us.

May Refrain.

OUR orchards wear a mantle white,
    Our fields with rainbow blooms are bright.
      So merrily smiles the May.
The missel thrush sings loud and clear
" Forsake your houses close and drear
      We'll all make holiday."

Too soon the hawthorn strews the walk,
The daffodil droops on tottering stalk ;
      So swiftly flies the May.
Soon blossoms fade and fruit grows ripe,
Soon autumn birds forget to pipe,
      Too short's our holiday.

Then come ! There's no excuse will fit,
The work of all must wait a bit ;
      So merrily smiles the May.
One joyous day 'neath summer skies,
Outweighs a world of care and sighs,
      We'll all make holiday.

To a Rose.

O BLEST above all roses,
    That on thy breast reposes,
  And gently heaves
  Its happy leaves,
  Like one afloat
  In an idle boat,
Who drifts and dreams and dozes!

I would not feel forsaken,
By kindly death o'ertaken,
  If, lulled to rest
  Upon thy breast,
  My heart might shed
  Each petal red,
And nevermore awaken.

One Word.

ONE little word I ask of thee,
    And do but say that word,
I'll mate it to a melody
    The sweetest ever heard.
My song so merry a tale shall tell,
    The birds will echo it pair by pair,
    The winds will carry it everywhere,
A-carolling down the dell.

One little word! And like a lute
    My heart will thrill again,
That needs must lie unstrung and mute
    If thou its chords disdain.
Then set the spirit of music free,
    To fill the heart of the world and mine,
    Oh! Let those roseate lips combine
    That word within a kiss to shrine,
And give the kiss to me!

Cherrybuds.

PINK buds upon the cherry,
   How long you've been asleep!
At last with dimple merry
   From out your hoods you peep.
So blithely you awaken,
   You cannot know at all
How soon, by showers shaken,
   Your petals frail will fall.

O Swift and Swallow fickle,
   We've waited for you still,
From days of sheaf and sickle,
   To days of daffodil!
The snowdrop lingered for you
   Long weeks of wintry gloom,
The tardy breeze that bore you
   Now sighs above her tomb.

But here comes one that's sweeter,
   Than break of April day;
The swallows haste to meet her
   The blossoms strew her way.
For she's my heart's own fairy,
   Whose spell outshines the sun;
His seasons shift and vary,
   Our summer's never done.

Regrets.

SMITTEN with frost and snow,
    April buds fail ;
Will winter never go,
    Summer prevail?

E'en though the greenwood wear
    Leaves as of yore,
Those that last May were fair
    Bud nevermore.

Say, can you love again,
    Poor heart of mine?
Is there for passion vain
    New summershine?

Haply some glimmer bright
    Cheers you and me ;
Not, with love's old delight,
Ever to pierce the night,
    —That cannot be.

At the Edge of the Sea.

SWIFTLY our boat has borne us down with the stream,
  We have drifted far in the day, my lover and I ;
The sunlit meadows of morning fade like a dream,
    And the night-cloud darkens the sky,
    For the end of our journey is nigh.

Longer the shadows fall on the cities of earth,
  Fainter the fevered clamour of market and street ;
The river is fuller, and deeper, and wider of girth,
    A sea-wind sings in the sheet,
    And the tide throbs under our feet.

Star of our love, undimmed by trouble and tears,
  Beacon of life thro' breaker, and shallow, and shoal,
Summon the lovers at last o'er the ocean of years
    To the unknown infinite goal,
    Unsundered in heart and soul.

Song of the Mavis.

SONG of the mavis,
 Wind from the heath,
How cheery thy stave is,
 How fresh is thy breath!

Blossoms on May-day
 Seem ever fair;
Love in his hey-day,
 What should he care?

Withered is the garland
 Of flowers you gave,
Love in a far land,
 True to the grave!

Song of the mavis,
 Wind from the heath,
How lonely the grave is,
 How bitter is death!

Sleep Little Soldiers.

SLEEP little soldiers of Christ the King,
   Safe through the darkness your slumber take ;
Sentinel angels are gathering,
   They shall keep vigil till morn doth break.

Vigilate custodes sereni ;
Dormite infantes terreni.

Wake with the dawn at the trumpet note,
   Life and its battle one day shall cease ;
Heavenward the shout of the host shall float,
   " Victory, triumph, eternal peace."

A Loyal Friend.

SOME sing their song of woman's love,
 Of war, and wine, and treasure trove,
   May heaven their ways amend !
But one thing most of all on earth
Will serve us best in grief or mirth,
A talisman of priceless worth,
   —A loyal friend.
Let hand grip hand, and side by side
   We'll laugh at doubt or fear ;
Firm as a rock we'll face the tide,
When trusty friends are near.

Like a beleagured company
We hold our own in jeopardy
   Within life's citadel ;
We joy to hear the trumpet blast
Of rescue come and danger past,
And hear the sentry call at last,
   "Pass friend, all's well."
Let hand grip hand, and side by side
   We'll laugh at doubt or fear ;
Firm as a rock we'll face the tide,
   When trusty friends are near.

Then fervent let the welcome be,
Whene'er the friendly face we see
    That's faithful to the end ;
A comfort when our need is most,
A life-boat on life's stormy coast,
This shall be aye our heartiest toast,
    —A loyal friend.
Let hand grip hand, and side by side
  We'll laugh at doubt or fear ;
Firm as a rock we'll face the tide,
  When trusty friends are near.

Ruth.

The evening wind blows cool in the wheat
  That whispers like river-rushes ;
The dove that crooned in the noonday heat,
  Her plaintive woodnote hushes.

I see you coming the cornfield way,
  Like Ruth in the old-world story ;
The ears bow down their homage to pay,
  As you pass in the sunset glory.

I loved you in days of new blade and leaf,
  With the green corn a spring month old ;
I would gather you now like a harvest sheaf,
  And bind you with a ring of gold !

Autumntide.

THE summer days are gone for aye,
  Their glamour still is here,
And gentle winds of autumn sigh
  Regretful of the year.
Dearer the ruddy leaves we knew
  In May's green livery,
And lovelier seem the flowers few
  That linger but to die.

The softest kisses of the sun
  Make twilight clouds to blush,
More gorgeous when the day is done
  The purple mountain's flush,
When decked in peerless panoply
  The nightwrack rides the air,
And, blazoned forth o'er land and sea,
  Makes dying day more fair.

Look up, beloved, in whose dear face
  Nor taint nor trace of time,
Nor shadow of night hath found a place,
  Nor touch of winter's rime!
Blest is the twilight of their day,
  Whose lips the night can move
To hymn their life's memorial lay
  In music of their love.

The Waterfall.

THE water springs so cool and clear
    And bubbles o'er the ledge ;
So fresh below the wild flowers grow
    That rim the water's edge !

One flower more beauteous than the rest
    Blooms near the waterfall ;
You, like that flower, are fairest, best,
    And most beloved of all.

The wavelet hastes to kiss her feet,
    By the brink of the new-born river,
As I would offer homage, Sweet,
    At your pure shrine for ever.

Sleeping and Waking.

THROUGHOUT the fragrant summer night
    I saw your face before me,
In plenitude of radiance bright,
Amid the regions of delight,
    Whereto my dreaming bore me.

And, stealing over each twin soul,
    A subtly-mingling essence,
Together drew in full control
Our lives to one harmonious whole,
    One undivided presence.

Now ere the lark from upward wing
    The beaded dew hath shaken,
From slumber-land for you I bring
The morning song I fain would sing,
    For you alone I waken.

The First Red Rose.

THE first red rose of summer is here,
    In the flush of full blown prime ;
The fragile flowers of April hours
    Are ghosts of a vanished time.

There is that within me draws my steps
    To the trelissed rosery near,
Where the buds of red like lamps o'erhead,
    In the dusk of the green leaves peer.

And if I give you the ruddiest rose,
    In crimson glory uncurled,
Oh! Take it as token of words unspoken,
    The bravest words in the world !

Since summer is chary of coming in,
    And hasty to fly away,
Since the rose of truelove 's best to win,
    We'll cherish it while we may.

The Fortunate Isle.

TELL me, where is the fortunate isle,
   Where the fabled garden of Hesperus stands?
It is over the ocean many a mile,
   Where the wave and the cloud join hands.

Whoever shall taste of the red fruit there,
   Grows void of sorrow and age they say,
But draws new life from that exquisite air,
   —Ah! Would we could know the way!—

If we only could know it, we'd soon take ship,
   And our happy keel hasten to kiss the shore,
Where the Sun-god's horses in ocean dip,
   When their day's long journey is o'er.

Then we'd sit together and sing at our ease,
   By the edge of the wood with the sea in view,
And gaze at the sky thro' the tangled trees,
   Forgetting the care we knew.

      I would never come back, would you?

Spring and Autumn.

THE shivering bird is silent
   Upon the leafless tree;
The pallid sun shines faintly
   Across the cheerless sea.

Is this the same sun glorious
   That dazed our eyes at noon?
Are these the green-clad branches
   With joyous birds attune?

Ah Love! Your smile's December,
   Where once your laugh was May;
Better to leave me mourning,
   Than, feigning love, to stay.

Four Maids at the Mill.

THERE are four pretty maids live down at the mill,
　　They are Nancy and Mary and Jane and Jill;
For seven long years have I known them there,
And I know none comlier anywhere.
　　　　And the mill goes round,
　　　　And the corn is ground,
　　But never a husband has one of them found.

Nancy 's an angel with eyes of blue,
And Mary 's as bright as a sunbeam too;
Jane is as lovely, but not so tall,
And Jill is the gem and the flower of them all.
　　　　And the mill goes round,
　　　　And the corn is ground,
　　But never a husband has one of them found.

Now the truth of the matter I think has been,
That Nancy has scarcely turned fourteen,
That Mary is twelve and Jane is eleven,
And dear little Jill is exactly seven.
　　　　And the mill goes round,
　　　　And the corn is ground,
　　And they'll all marry some day, I'll be bound!

Rustic Philosophy.

THE dew in the morn
　　Hangs thick on the thorn,
The midsummer day 's quite young ;
　　And dairyman Dick
　　Goes clatter click click,
His pails from his shoulders slung.
　　" If ladies in silk
　　Drank morning milk
And lived less hurly-burly,
　　They wouldn't look done
　　At thirty-one
And go to their grave so early.

　　" Now, Marion, you
　　Milk crumpled Sue,
While I milk Strawberry Roan ;
　　And we'll pray for our life,
　　Both man and wife,
That the great folk leave us alone ;
　　The ladies in satin
　　That sing Greek and Latin
To the young Lords up at the Hall,
　　Know nought of the charm
　　Of a dairy farm,
Nor the pleasures of life at all."

Evening.

THE sun sinks lower
    Behind the tower,
  The red light shines in the west;
The ocean is calm,
    The land is at rest,
And love's soft balm
    Steals over my breast.

The seagulls hover,
The waves uncover
    The golden sands in the bay;
The wind sings gladly,
    "Away, away,"
My love cries madly,
    "To-day, to-day!"

Wintertide.

THE snow falls, not a wind doth sigh,
    All things are hushed to-night ;
And steadily and stealthily
    The land is lapped in white.

On roof and field and whitening trees
    The countless snowflakes fall,
Like swarms of silent silver bees,
    That settle and cover all.

And gazing out on the wintry plain,
    My heart grows desolate too,
Like some poor bird that seeks in vain
    The summer fields it knew.

I only long to hear one word
    From a voice lost long ago,
More musical than sleigh bells heard
    Across the frozen snow.

How lonely is the still cold night,
    Come back one hour to me !
Speak once again my life's delight !
    Ah No ! That cannot be.

The Nightingale.

THE nightingale has taken flight
   Through heaven's unguarded portal,
And come to bless our world to-night
   With melody immortal.

Anon a woodnote low and mild,—
   And trees lean down to learn his story;
Anon a pæan, exultant, wild,
   Floods earth and air with rhythmic glory.

On such a night can love be dumb?
Rejoice! The nightingale has come!

His echo in the river is heard,
   He sets the brown bee humming;
He sets the tune to every bird,
   The flowers unfold at his coming.

Such hope newborn he caroleth,
   Such promise brave of summer weather,
That everything with bud or breath
   Must fain grow jubilant together.

O heart of hearts can love be dumb?
Rejoice! The nightingale is come!

The First Leaf has Fallen.

THE first leaf has fallen,
　　The first swallow gone;
Too short is the twilight,
As autumn draws on.

Yet, hark, in yon woodland
Above the wind's sigh,
I hear one bird singing
A brave melody!

His song's bright with beauty
Of joys gone before,
Like the last ray of sunset
The last glimpse of shore.

For he seems to say, "Mourn not
The leaf-widowed wood;
Only remember
How summer was good."

Your Voice.

THE worst of the winter is over,
   The worst of the snow and the rain,
And the songs of the lark and the plover
   Rise clear o'er the meadows again.
Then welcome the voice of my lover,
   Outvieing their strain.

'Tis the wash of the waves on the shingle,
   Whose lullaby murmur I hear;
'Tis the ripple of the rill in the dingle,
   And the wind wafted over the mere.
How sweetly their melodies mingle
   When your voice is near!

Then grant me by day to be near it,
   Let it float through my dreams in the night,
Till it ravish my soul like a spi it
   And tune all my being aright,
For ever and ever to hear it
   In endless delight!

Morning Song.

THE leaves are lightly shaken,
    The lulled wind stirs and sighs.
My Lady-love awaken,
    My Love, arise, arise!

The flowers that throng your garden
    In dutiful array,
Would never grant me pardon
    If I let their Queen delay.

Your vassal birds assemble,
    Expectant all and dumb,
Their tuneful throats a-tremble
    To greet you when you come.

The world seems all forsaken
    Until you open your eyes;
My Lady-love awaken,
    My Love, arise, arise!

Seed and Flower.

THE seed a bird let fall
   Upon my garden bed,
Sprang up the loveliest flower of all
   By rain and sunshine fed.

The sigh that from me fell,
   Impalpable as air,
Found favour where my heart would dwell,
   And touched my lady fair.

I plucked the flower full-blown,
   And laid it on her breast,
And lady and flower were both mine own,
   And so my heart found rest.

Mirth and Sorrow.

'TWAS heedless happy April-tide
  When Sorrow first sought earth,
Where all was lapped in careless pride
  Of unsuspecting Mirth.

Then Sorrow came with care and crime,
  With wind and hail and gloom;
Men failed of life before their prime,
  And buds before their bloom.

But while the world stood sad and still,
  And Mirth had ta'en to flight,
Love came with counsel and goodwill
  To set the trouble right.

He mated Mirth and Sorrow there,
  In April sun and rain,
An equal share of life to bear,
  —And the world went on again.

False Love and True.

THE false love that I loved so well,
   The true love that loved me ;
How foolish hearts may suffer !
   How cruel love can be !

Like will-o'-the wisp she led my steps,
   The love I loved the best,
With treacherous light through murky night ;
   And still I found no rest.

My true love, like the evening star,
   Shone bright and clear and true ;
She never paled nor wavered,
   Yet I no comfort knew.

Till, bruised and wounded shamefully,
   My false love mocked my pain,
But my true love smiled in tenderness,
And woke my heart from sore distress
   To life and love again.

In Treeland.

UP in merry treeland yonder
    Fairies come and go,
Through the greenwood world they wander,
    Flitting to and fro.

When the old treetop is swinging,
    And the wind blows fair,
You may hear their happy singing
    Echo through the air.

Hush ! 'Neath leafy roof and rafter
    Rolls the sound along,
—Melody of tuneful laughter ;—
    Harken to their song !

Within My Heart.

WITHIN my heart is a palace,
  Kept ever fresh and fair,
Where all but hallowed visions
And tender thoughts forbear;
There may I still the gladness know
That filled my life long years ago.

I open the door and enter,
A warm light glows within,
The years of pain and sorrow
Dissolve to phantoms thin;
I see the face that heaven had sent
To make my longing soul content.

Hope sets his star above us,
Love folds his wings around,
Two voices blent together
Make sweet harmonious sound.
—Oh! Shatter not the dream divine
That makes one hour of rapture mine!

The Freaks of Love.

WHERE can a maid a true love find?
    This world it is most hollow,
She needs must have a supple mind
    The freaks of love would follow.

The first that woo'd me sighed and swore
    His heart for love was crazy;
But when he knew my lot was poor,
    His love grew cold and lazy.

Yet gladly did I smile and sing
    To greet the next new-comer,
And he was faithful all the spring,
    But left me in the summer.

Heigh Ho! Why love should treat me so
    I never can discover,
Faith! I shall break my heart with woe,
    —Or seek another lover!

Good and Ill.

WILD flowers of folly springing where we walk,
In youth most sweet of savour, short of stalk ;
How soon they wither in hand !

Rank weeds of ruth in eld that kneedeep grow,
With clinging burrs that hinder as we go,
Stiff in our way they stand.

Yet in my pilgrimage I'll not complain,
Culling of herbs and simples for heart's bane,
Where no cure lies, I wis ;

Both good and ill I'll suffer as each grows,
Since each for use on Earth I must suppose
While Earth my country is.

Fancy's Journey.

WILL you come sailing on yonder cloud,
    Westward, away in the twilight glow?
Steering along in our galleon proud
Thro' the amber gates where the sunset waits,
    To the blue beyond we'll go.

We'll cast our cloudlet adrift in air,
And land and clamber the starry stair,
    Step by step to the height serene
    Where never a cloud nor a bird has been;
Will you follow me upward there?

Then mounting the car of the silver moon,
    So merrily round the world we'll ride,
In the beautiful kingdom where night is noon,
Rocked half asleep where the angels croon
    In harmony glorified.

And if it be fancy that set the tune,
Ah! Let us not flutter to earth too soon!

Thoughts of Summer.

WHAT thoughts the budding year brings in
    When the lark soars high o'er the fallow !
The longer sunnier days begin,
    And the whistling waggoner halts his team
    To cool their feet in the bubbling stream
By meadows of gold marsh-mallow.

'Twas yesteryear in daffodil days
  I loved you first completely,
    In hawthorn time I dared to woo,
    In rosetide won your heart from you ;
Three merrier months ne'er went their ways
  Linked hand in hand so sweetly.

To sigh by stealth for worldly wealth
  Were mean and pitiful treason ;
    Of grosser coin tho' small my share,
    My love's a treasure past compare,
    That jewel next my heart I'll wear
For many a summer season.

The Golden Age.

WOULD you, old earth again
    The golden age could see,
When nature's every nook confessed
    Some present deity?

What if the nymphs yet danced
    On daisy-spangled lawns,
'Mid woods and hills made musical
    By laughter-loving fauns?

Doth trembling Daphne now
    Yon rustling laurel haunt?
Yon plaintive strain of nightingale
    Doth Philomela chaunt?

Lurk not a thousand sprites
    In stream and wood and hill?
If so it was in golden age,
    Perchance it is so still.

First and Best.

WHEN winter leaves the frozen north
    And wood-anemonies peep forth,
More prized than summer's lordliest hour
The advent of the first-born flower.

On welcome wing the swallow hies
From sunny climes to cloudy skies;
We hail with joy the pilgrim host,
But love the earliest comer most.

O Love, whose spell we sweetest own,
Like bird or flower when newly known,
Though later loves the heart enthrall,
Our hidden tears the first recall!

Children's Rhyme.

WHEN the logs were burning bright,
    And the frost was hoar,
Daddy Winter came one night
    Knocking at our door.

We took him in and cared for him,
    Poor old shivering soul!
We chafed and warmed each frozen limb,
    And spiced the wassail bowl.

So for months we let him stay,
    Housed and fed him well,
Till at last one April day
    Strange events befel.

Through the window, opened wide,
    Golden sunlight shone;
There was saucy Spring inside,
    Daddy Winter gone!

Storm and Sunshine.

WHEN winter seas are drear and dun,
And scudding clouds obscure the sun,
The wave that dashes on the rock
Is spurned and shattered by the shock.
    So is my heart a stormy sea,
    When thou art cold to me.

How gently tides of summer flow
In sunny seas where no winds blow!
The blue waves dimple o'er the sand,
And softly sighing kiss the land.
    So is my heart a summer sea
    When thou art kind to me.

O Love of mine, in storm or shine
My constant heart shall cling to thine;
    There like the sea upon the shore
    To throb for evermore.

The Time for Wooing.

WHEN hill and dale look merriest in May,
    And winter frosts are well away,
With every tree in proud array
    His brave green coat renewing,
When bluebells bloom on the daffodil's tomb,
    Why! Then's the time for wooing!

When summer's come and come to stay,
When strawberries ripen day by day,
And every hand's gone down to the hay,
    With a cheer the last load carrying,
When cuckoo's tune is changed with June,
    Why! Then's the time for marrying!

When years drift on and hair grows grey,
When cares and sorrows sometimes weigh,
And little ones grow grave or gay
    At praising or reproving,
With faithful mate and heart elate,
    Life-long's the time for loving.

A Fairy Tale.

WHEN fairies through the flowers flit,
    And tipple crystal dew,
I love beneath the stars to sit,
    And tell my tale to you.

        It was a fairy maid of old
            That loved a mortal man,
        But loved to tease his heart of gold
            As only fairies can.

        Each night he sought her as she fled,
            By forest, flood and field,
        And beckoning still and still ahead
            Her tiny laughter pealed.

        Till wandering where the millstream flows,
            All faint and weary grown,
        A water nymph in pity rose
            And drew him gently down.

        And still above the millwheel's note
            You hear the nymph's glad strain;
        While in a water-lily boat
            The fairy weeps in vain.

Oh! Mourn her fate and think on it,
    Sweet maid with eyes of blue,
As here beneath the stars I sit
    And tell my tale to you.

Brief Sojourners.

YON leaf again we shall not see,
   That spreads upon the chestnut tree,
Nor hear again yon songster sing
That carols in the opening spring;
For leaf and bird will fly away
Some bitter bleak autumnal day.

And can our hearts that beat in tune
Forever laugh from June to June?
Can we one fleeting hour recall,
Although our love is all in all?
Nay! After few or many years,
True love itself must part in tears.

Dream and Song.

YOU came like a vision bright
   That leaves not the wakening sleeper,
You filled my life with delight
   Of love growing deeper and deeper.

You come as a song sublime
   Comes once to the minstrel enchanted,
'Tis his to the ending of time,
   Though none such another is granted.

You came like the summertide
   To a world all weary of waiting,
When leaves in the wood spread wide,
   When birds make busy with mating.

And full of the summer our lives shall be,
For the dream and the song have come true for me.

Good Night, All.

WELL! Good night all! Our songs are sung,
    The curfew bell long time has rung,
Let merry minstrels, old and young,
    Say " Lullaby, sleep well."

Let drowsy head make no demur
To sheets long laid in lavender,
But slumber sound, and never stir ;
    So Lullaby, sleep well.

And when the midnight hour shall toll,
Let no ill thought disturb your soul,
Nor nightmare nag your brain control
    And weave infernal spell.

Avaunt! Hobgoblin demon wights!
Avaunt! Banshees that howl o'nights,
With gibbering elemental sprites
    And fiends let loose from hell!

Haste, fairies fresh from Morpheus' hill,
On lip and eyelid to distil
Kind poppy juice, and with good-will
    Sing "Lullaby, sleep well."

Now then to bed in peace we'll go,
May dreams as pure as virgin snow
Our limbs refresh till cock doth crow.
    So "Lullaby, sleep well."

www.ingramcontent.com/pod-product-compliance
Lightning Source LLC
Chambersburg PA
CBHW032149160426
43197CB00008B/838